Spinning Tops

Story by Jan Anderson
Photography by Lindsay Edwards

Rigby®

A Harcourt Achieve Imprint

www.Rigby.com
1-800-531-5015

One Saturday morning,

Jimmy came to see his friend Ramon.

"Hi, Ramon," said Jimmy.

"I have a present for you."

Ramon looked in the bag.

"It's a spinning top," he said.

"It's like the one we saw on TV."

"Yes," said Jimmy,

"I have one, too.

We can play a game with them."

"Where can we spin the tops?"
said Jimmy.

The boys looked around the room.

"Let's spin them on the carpet,"
said Ramon.
"That will be a good place."

"We can't spin the tops
on the carpet," said Jimmy.
"Look! They get stuck
and won't go around."

"We can spin them
on this table," said Ramon.

But Ramon's top went so fast
that it went spinning
off the table.

"This is not a very good place,"
said Ramon.

Jimmy said to Ramon's mom,
"The tops won't spin on the carpet,
and they spin off the table."

"Where can we play our game, Mom?"
said Ramon.

"You can spin your tops
on this big tray," said Mom.

"Thanks, Mom," said Ramon.
"They won't come off the tray.
Now we can have some fun."

14

"The first one over this line
is the winner," said Jimmy.

"Look at them go!" shouted Ramon.